SUNSET AT FIERY INFERNO
Arches National Park, Utah

BIRCH TREES AND FALL COLOR

New Hampshire

VISIONS OF NATURE

A Portfolio of Images of our Natural World

Photography by Bill La Brie
Introduction by Richard Garrod

SUNRISE MONUMENT VALLEY
Navajo Tribal land, Utah/Arizona

Title page image detail from page 35

Highland Press
222 Jewell Street
San Rafael, California 94901
Designed by Bill La Brie and Joanne Bolton

ISBN: 0-9662414-2-8

First printing limited to twelve hundred and fifty copies plus
fifty editions each slipcased and presented with a limited edition print, signed and numbered.

Printed in Hong Kong through
Bolton Associates, Inc., San Rafael, CA

DEDICATION

This book is dedicated to my wife Cyndie,

who has been with me from the beginning of my

journey into photography. She has been patient on many occasions

while I was waiting for the right light, or searching

for the perfect tree.

ROCKS AND SURF
Big Sur, California

FOREWORD

My first thoughts of photography were in 1967 when I was in the Navy and I borrowed a 35mm camera from a friend. I had a great time photographing at the local botanical gardens and imagining that I was a professional photographer, but this only lasted a brief time. Photography did not enter my life again until 1980, when my wife and I went on a backpack trip to the bottom of the Grand Canyon. If you have never ventured into the canyon, you simply cannot appreciate how spectacular it is. I brought along a little Kodak instamatic camera and spent a lot of time photographing the beauty of the Canyon. I saw many other hikers with big 35mm cameras and assumed that I was going to get the same quality of pictures with my little 110 camera.

When I returned home and got my images back, I was very disappointed. What had inspired me in the canyon, I thought I would see in my little 3x5 prints. However, my pictures were flat and lifeless. What had happened? Was it a processing error? When I would show those images to my friends, I kept hearing myself say, "It was really more spectacular than what you see here." It was at that time I decided to learn how to make images that reconnected me with my adventures.

I purchased my first 35mm camera and started my journey into photography. I researched photography books of masters like Ansel Adams, Elliot Porter, Edward Weston and Phillip Hyde. These artists were dedicated to their art and to the environment. I learned that photography is a powerful tool to inform people of our environment and its need for protection. Being self-taught, my progress at times seemed like one step forward and two steps back. However, I never gave in to the frustration that can happen to you when you are learning on your own. Over time, I became aware that my transparencies were beginning to reveal my vision and that people were inspired by my images. My change from 35mm to medium format and then to 4x5 helped me to refine my personal style. The 4x5 is a wonderful tool and I use it faithfully. Since using the large format camera is a slower process, it allows me to be more selective about my images. The experience of being out in the environment is not just getting *The Image*, it's about getting there, who I'm with and the time of year. This is all part of the great adventure of photography.

Mother Nature, the greatest artist of all, is not always easy to put on film. When light and composition come together I feel engaged, and the magic of the moment inspires me. Sometimes to get the great image, it's being in the right place at the right time. At other times, it takes careful planning to get the image, and I may have to return time after time looking for that elusive light.

I hope that those who view my images will have the feeling of being there; being able to walk into an image and feel as though you are there. It can be very inspiring. We are at a point in time when we need our natural world to remind us of who we are. Our planet is a very beautiful yet fragile place, and photographic images can enhance our awareness of that.

As you travel through my book of images, I hope that they bring you peace and inspiration, just as they did for me when I captured them.

Preserve the spirit of our natural world

Bill La Brie

CRACKED MUD ON SAND DUNES
Death Valley, California

WILDFLOWERS AT SHELL CREEK

Coastal Foothills, California

INTRODUCTION

Bill La Brie's rich color photographs reveal a keen and uncompromising eye and a long dedication to the demanding process and traditions of fine art photography. They define an inner realm of awareness and a unique sensitivity to the interplay of color, space, form, and especially light. Bill has had a devotion to the beauty of the photographic medium, nurtured by nearly three decades of work. He has spent his time honing a keen eye and developing his inner intuitive self. The synergy between the boldness of his inspired vision and his skillful technical expertise has results in images of eloquence, subtlety, and insight, as displayed in this long awaited book.

I met Bill five years ago, when we were guests at a Chuck Farmer Workshop in Lone Pine on the east side of the Sierra Nevada Mountains. We worked together for nearly a week and I was deeply impressed with his ability at personal exploration and visual discovery. His images were always "well seen" and succeeded in a transformation of the objects of his vision that revealed the depths and force behind his seeing. It is the artist's goal to be able to transcend the outer object and emotionally capture an internal attitude or feeling that conveys the inner spirit of the person behind the camera. Over the years of perfecting his work, Bill has mastered this goal of transformation and keeps it uppermost in his mind as he continually seeks the message behind the landscape.

Bill spent many years developing his technical expertise, having worked with a variety of formats and types of equipment. He is a master of readiness, being quick to seize visual opportunities. He captures the constant rhythm and ceaseless change of the natural scene, and with no hesitancy despite the technical challenges that are always involved. His devotion to what he calls "nature, the greatest artist of all," is uppermost in his mind, as he works fluidly and with great introspection. The resulting images provide a thread that unifies the inner and outer worlds of his psyche, forever locked in silver, for all to appreciate and enjoy.

Richard Garrod
Monterey, 2005

Richard Garrod is a respected photographer on the Monterey Peninsula, California. He has worked with Ansel Adams, Brett Weston, Minor White and many other fine photographers. He has had more than fifty solo and group exhibitions. His latest book, Visual Prayers, published by the Monterey Museum of Art, is a collection of exquisite black & white images.

LUPINE IN SPRING
Eastern Sierra, California

SUNSET WITH STREAM AT LOW TIDE

Central Coast, California

PINES IN FOG

Cambria, California

LUPINE IN SPRING
Cambria, Central Coast, California

It was a hard country, nothing nice or

comfortable about it,

It was only gorgeous.

Rob Schulteis

SUNRISE AT MESA ARCH

Canyonlands, Utah

ASPEN IN FALL

McGee Creek, Sierra Nevada, California

SUNRISE ON THE COURT

Zion National Park, Utah

CYPRESS TREES
Point Lobos, Carmel, California

ANTELOPE CANYON
Arizona

KELSO DUNES

Mojave Preserve, California

HEDGEHOG CACTUS AND SPRING GRASS

Anza Borrego State Park, California

I am usually very calm

over the displays of Nature,

but you will scarce believe

how my heart leaped at this....

It was like meeting one's wife,

I had come home again.

Robert Louis Stevenson

SUNSET ON EL CAPITAN
Yosemite, California

BEE HIVES AND BAKED BUNS

Paria Wilderness, Arizona

THE SUBWAY
Zion National Park, Utah

OAK TREE IN FALL NEAR EL CAPITAN

Yosemite Valley, California

FALL LEAVES AND CREEK
Sierra Nevada Foothills, California

CASCADE ON NORTH CREEK

Zion National Park, Utah

WILDFLOWERS
Table Mountain, California

The finest workers in stone

are not copper or steel tools,

but gentle touches of air and water

working at their leisure

with liberal allowances of time.

Henry David Thoreau

PARIA CANYON
Coyote Buttes, Arizona

LIQUID GOLD SUNSET

Central Coast, California

WINTER ASPEN
Zion National Park, Utah

TOWERS OF SILENCE

Desert, Southwest Utah

WHITNEY PORTAL
High Sierra, California

OCEAN WATERFALL

Julia Pfeiffer Burns State Park, California

ROCKS AND POOLS, LOW TIDE
Central Coast, California

SUNSET ON THE SOUTH RIM

We simply need that wild country

available to us, even if we never

do more than drive to its' edge and look in.

Wallace Stegner

BURNEY FALLS
Northern California

WINTER SUNSET
Cambria, California

RETURN CREEK

High Sierra, California

WINTER SUNSET

Cambria, California

RETURN CREEK

High Sierra, California

ASPEN IN SNOW
Lake Tahoe, California

YOUNG SAPLING, MERCED RIVER
Yosemite Valley, California

Time is a flowing river. Happy those who

allow themselves to be carried, unresisting,

with the current. They float through easy days.

They live unquestioning in the moment.

Christopher Morley

COTTONWOOD BASIN
High Sierra, California

SUNRISE ON FALL TREES
Smoky Mountains, Tennessee

FALL IN THE SAN JUAN MOUNTAINS

San Juan Mountains, Colorado

SUNRISE AT EAGLE FALLS
Lake Tahoe, California

ROCK WALL AND SNAG

Zion National Park, Utah

SHELL CREEK MEADOW
Coastal Mountains, California

To be poor and not have trees is to be

the most starved human in the world.

To be poor and to have trees is to be

completely rich in ways that money

can never buy.

Clarissa Estes

PRIMROSE A
Anza Borrego S

NATURE'S GARDEN
Yankee Boy Basin, Colorado

SUNRISE
Portage Glacier, Alaska

SUNRISE AT RED MOUNTAIN PASS
San Juan Mountains, Colorado

CASCADE WATERFALL
Yosemite Valley, California

PINE TREE AND ASPEN IN FALL
McGee Creek, High Sierra, California

When people talk to me about

my photography, I tell them

I'm not patient, I'm persistent.

Bill La Brie

When one tugs at a single

thing in Nature, he finds it

attached to the rest of the world.

John Muir

OLD MAN'S BEARD

MORNING LIGHT AT BADWATER
Death Valley, California

WHITE HOUSE

Canyon De Chelly, Arizona

FLOWERS AND WATERFALL
San Juan Mountains, Colorado

EAGLE FALLS

Lake Tahoe, California

EL CAPITAN REFLECTION
Yosemite Valley, California

ROCK TOWER FAMILY

Desert Southwest, Utah

PARIA CANYON
Coyote Buttes, Arizona

THE WATCHMEN AT SUNSET
Zion National Park, Utah

It's all about the light.

Bill La Brie

CARSON PASS

High Sierra, California

OAKS AND THUNDER CLOUDS
Santa Lucia Mountains, California

FALL COLOR
Vermont

GRASS VALLEY POPPIES
Sierra Foothills, California

I frequently tramped eight or ten miles

through the deepest snow to keep an

appointment with a beech tree, or a

yellow birch, or an old

acquaintance among the pines.

Henry David Thoreau

OAKS IN SNOW STORM

SILVER CASCADE

New Hampshire

SHEEP MOUNTAIN, FIRE WEED
Chugach Mountains, Alaska

FALL COLOR
New Hampshire

COLUMBINE, SAN JUAN MOUNTAINS
Yankee Boy Basin, Colorado

SUNRISE, EMERALD BAY

There are times at sunrise or sunset

when the light is so perfect that my camera

becomes more important than other comforts in life.

Bill La Brie

SACRED KIVA
Utah

ANTELOPE CANYON
Arizona

LIME KILN STATE PARK
Big Sur Coast, California

STORM SURF
Central Coast, California

SMUGGLERS' COVE

Central Coast, California

ICEBERG IN MORNING SUN
Inland Passage, Alaska

Nature does not hurry,

yet everything is accomplished.

Lao Tzu

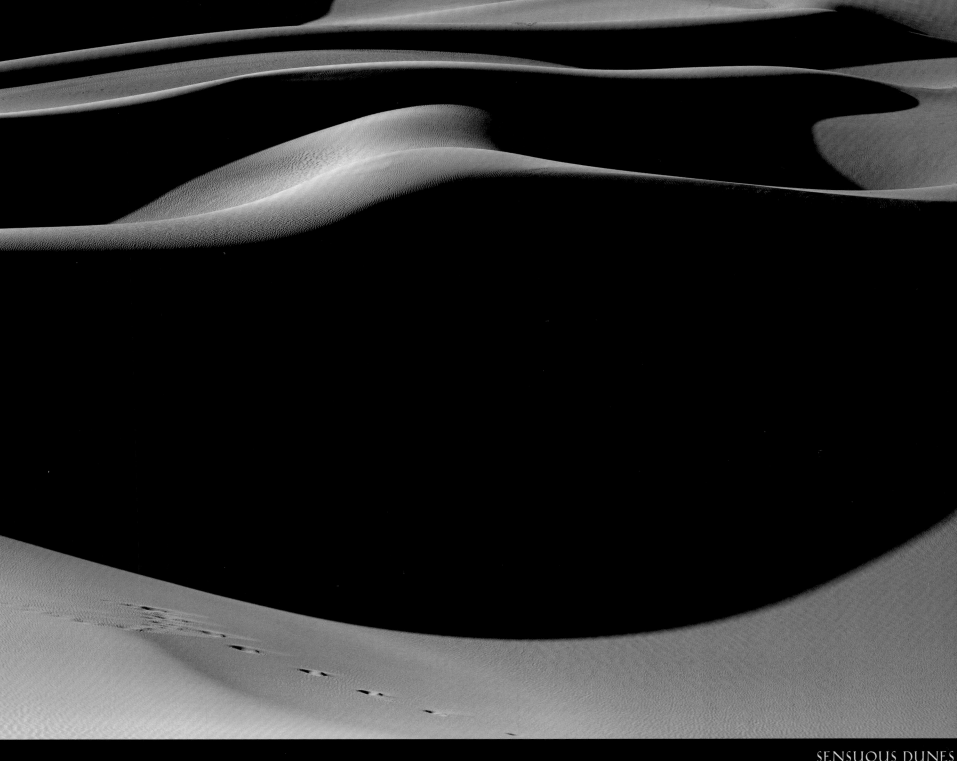

SENSUOUS DUNES

SAND DUNES AT SUNSET

Death Valley, California

TIDE POOL
Central Coast, California

"Simplicity, simplicity,

simplicity."

Henry David Thoreau

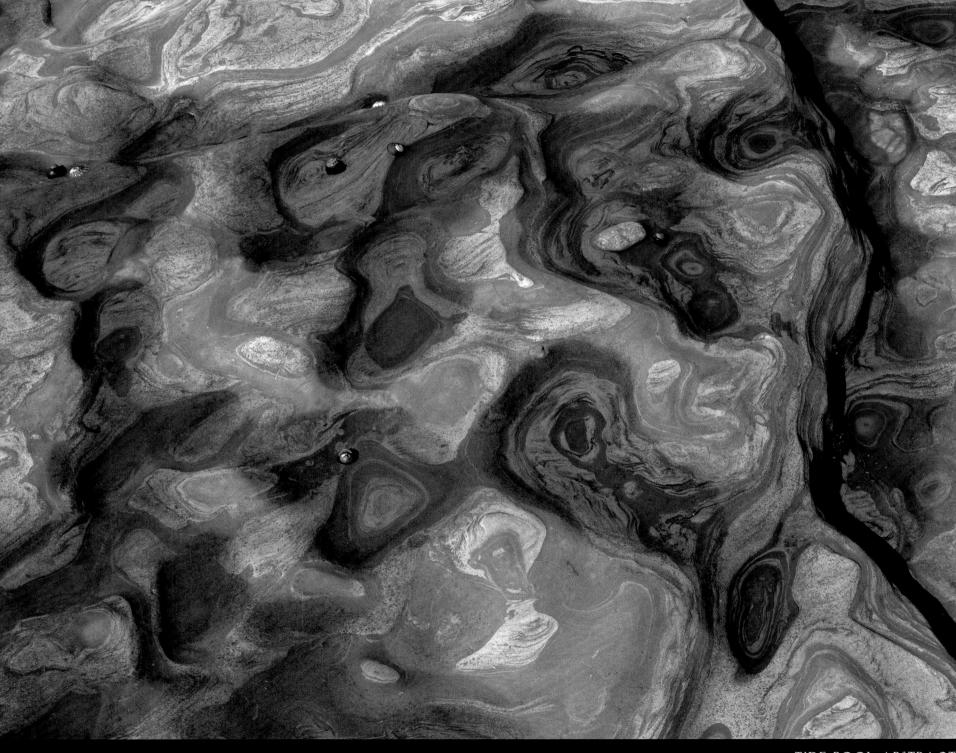

TIDE POOL ABSTRACT

THREE BROTHERS AT SUNRISE
Yosemite, California

HALF DOME RISING

Yosemite National Park, California

The difference between landscape and landscape is small,
but there is a great difference between the beholders.

Ralph Waldo Emerson

STORM SURF, MOONSTONE BEACH

LUPINE AND POPPIES

Grass Valley, California

THE DANCE
Wasatch Mountains, Utah

And God said, "Let there be Light!"

The Bible: Genesis 1:3

LAST RAYS

TUNNEL VIEW AT SUNSET

Yosemite Valley, California

CARPET OF FLOWERS
Shell Creek, Coastal Foothills, California

ACKNOWLEDGEMENTS

How do I begin to thank all the people that in one way or another over the years have helped me in my photography? A special thanks to Megg McNamee; without her support my book would not have happened. In addition, I would like to thank Richard Garrod for the Introduction, Bill and Eric at Laser Light for doing the scans and for all the great prints they have made for me, Ann Grossman and Lillian Gleicher for making sure the text was correct, John Weldon for all the beautiful cibachromes over the years and Joanne Bolton for helping me put this book together.

I want to thank all my friends who have supported my photography and who have always given me words of encouragement. Thank you to the ones I helped and inspired on their photographic journeys. They have inspired me to be a better photographer, and in their own way, have become mentors for me.

ROCKS AND SURF
Garrapata, California

NOTES ON PHOTOGRAPHY

Excellent nature photography reveals an emotional attachment between photographer and subject matter; nature photographers love nature and know her sensuality. Photography is a large percent seeing and the rest photographing, you just cannot photograph it if you don't see it! Good nature photography is a way of life and a state of mind; you have to want the image and be willing to put out the effort and be persistent in your pursuit for that which moves you.

Many of my images are taken when it's raining or when the weather is bad. There are times when I'm tired and hungry and have been out all day and want to go back to my camp or motel room and rest, but my duty to the camera comes first, and that's when I get some of my best images.

It's always nice to know the equipment that a photographer uses; excellent images can be taken with all formats and we should never think that a certain camera would make us better photographers.

I photograph with a large format Toyo 45A with lenses 75mm, 90mm, 135mm, 210mm, 360mm, & 500mm. This is my main camera of choice, it's a tool that works best for me. For my panoramic images, I use a Horseman 6x12 back. I also use a Pentax 6x7 medium format camera with lenses from 45mm to 300mm. My choice of film is Ektachrome VS, Fuji Velvia, and Provia in 4x5 & 6x7 format.

DESCRIPTIONS

1 SUNSET AT FIERY INFERNO
ARCHES NATIONAL PARK, UTAH
I really enjoy photographing this part of Utah. Moab is a great town to have as a base for exploring Canyonlands and Arches. This image is in Arches at a place called the Fiery Inferno. I loved the old snag in the foreground. I went back many years later but couldn't find the snag.
Toyo 45A   90mm lens

2 BIRCH TREES AND FALL COLOR
NEW HAMPSHIRE
This area was in a canyon with a river running through it. It was very green and the trees were in full fall foliage. I liked the texture of the birch with the brilliant colors behind.
Toyo 45A   90mm lens

4 SUNRISE MONUMENT VALLEY
NAVAJO TRIBAL LANDS, UTAH/ARIZONA
Toyo 45A   90mm lens

6 ROCKS AND SURF
BIG SUR, CALIFORNIA
This image shows how light and composition can really change an image. I photographed this in the summer near sunset about 8:30 pm. The other image of this exact spot (P. 110) was photographed in the winter at 4:30 pm. They each have their own look and feel, vertical versus horizontal and warm summer light versus cooler winter light.
Toyo 45A   360mm lens

9 CRACKED MUD ON SAND DUNES
DEATH VALLEY, CALIFORNIA
I always like the cracked mud on the sand dunes at Stovepipe Wells. This particular year there were a few areas where it was just right; not a lot of foot traffic destroying it. It's almost like the back of a giant turtle.
Toyo 45A   90mm lens

10 WILDFLOWERS AT SHELL CREEK
COASTAL FOOTHILLS, CALIFORNIA
2005 was a very wet year and wildflowers were everywhere. I took a seventeen hundred mile trip through the deserts in search of flowers, but I think the best displays were here, only a little over an hour from home.
Toyo 45A   90mm lens

12 LUPINE IN SPRING, (COVER)
EASTERN SIERRA, CALIFORNIA
I think this field of lupine is one of the most spectacular I have ever seen. A ranger in Lone Pine had told me that there were lupine at this location, so I decided to check it out. When I got there I was so excited I couldn't get out of my car fast enough. I had to go back three times before I finally got the right combination of light and clouds.
Toyo 45A   90mm lens

13 SUNSET WITH STREAM AT LOW TIDE
CENTRAL COAST, CALIFORNIA
I have a good opportunity to be in the right position for sunset images, as I live just down the highway from this beach. The stream of water only appears after a rainstorm, and has a different pattern every time.
Toyo 45A   90mm lens

14 PINES IN FOG
CAMBRIA, CALIFORNIA
I worked hard at getting this image. As I do not live far, it was easy for me to keep my eye on it. I wanted some fog and more contrast between the trees and the ground. When the grass dried out and we started to get some fog, it all came together.
Toyo 45A   210mm lens

15 LUPINE IN SPRING
CAMBRIA, CENTRAL COAST, CALIFORNIA
The purple lupine this year were incredible; the years before there were none. Only a little ways from my home, I waited for an overcast sky and no wind.
Toyo 45A   90mm lens

17 SUNRISE AT MESA ARCH
CANYONLANDS, UTAH
This is a very popular image with photographers and has been photographed many times in many different compositions. It was very good for me this particular morning. This light only happens at sunrise. It was May and the sun's position at this time of year and a little haze made the arch look like hot lava.
Toyo 45A   90mm lens

18 ASPEN IN FALL
McGEE CREEK, SIERRA NEVADA, CALIFORNIA
Fall in the High Sierra is always beautiful. This grove of aspen was lit up by a thin overcast sky making the colored leaves pop.
Toyo 45A   360mm lens

19 SUNRISE ON THE COURT
ZION NATIONAL PARK, UTAH
The Court of The Patriarchs presides over the Virgin River in Zion. This image was at sunrise. The clouds from a weather front softened the light on the towers and made a nice reflection on the river.
Toyo 45A   90mm lens

20 CYPRESS TREES
POINT LOBOS, CARMEL, CALIFORNIA
It was spring and everything was brilliant green. The sky was like a big diffuser; the grays of the snags and the green trees contrasted with each other creating two images in one. This is one of my favorites.
Toyo 45A   360mm lens

21 ANTELOPE CANYON
ARIZONA,
The tumbleweed fell in the crack while we were photographing; it was not there when we arrived. I waited for it to light up and got my image. The light only lasted for a short time. These canyons have become a favorite destination for many photographers.
Toyo 45A   210mm lens

22 KELSO DUNES
MOJAVE PRESERVE, CALIFORNIA
I hiked the dunes looking for wildflowers but finding very few. Near the top of the dunes I spotted these grasses and liked the combination of grass, white sand and deep blue sky.
Toyo 45A   90mm lens

23 HEDGEHOG CACTUS AND SPRING GRASS
ANZA BORREGO STATE PARK, CALIFORNIA
This is the most grass that I have ever seen in the park in spring; it was two feet tall in some places. The wind was howling so I just let the grass move and focused on the great blooms on the cactus.
Toyo 45A   75mm lens

25 SUNSET ON EL CAPITAN
YOSEMITE, CALIFORNIA
Whenever I am in Yosemite Valley I visit this location. I previsualize this image, but most of the time it never materializes. This winter when I was in the valley, it had been snowing off and on all day and I figured that my spot would be socked in. I went anyway and set up my camera, and to my surprise, the clouds opened and a band of gold light lit up El Capitan. As the sun went lower, so did the band of light until the Merced River turned gold. With the last of the light I was able to get my image. Of all the shots I took, this was the only one that had gold in the river.
Toyo 45A   90mm lens

26 BEE HIVES AND BAKED BUNS
PARIA WILDERNESS, ARIZONA
There are so many images in this area but a lot of attention goes to one place called The Wave. I thought the rocks here were really great but the light was starting to fade. I only got two images before it was too dark on the Bee Hives in the background. I will return here again and spend my time again outside The Wave .
Toyo 45A   90mm lens

27 THE SUBWAY
ZION NATIONAL PARK, UTAH
The Subway is approximately a ten mile round-trip hike on North Creek in Zion. A tough hike for me, carrying about 45 pounds of large-format gear, but worth it. I would like to go back.
Toyo 45A   75mm lens

28 OAK TREE IN FALL NEAR EL CAPITAN
YOSEMITE VALLEY, CALIFORNIA
I was in Yosemite Valley for the fall color. The oaks in October can be anywhere from bright yellow to gold. I was looking for an oak with the wall of El Capitan behind it. This design was just what I was looking for.
Toyo 45A   360mm lens

29 FALL LEAVES AND CREEK
SIERRA NEVADA FOOTHILLS, CALIFORNIA
When I was living in the Sierra Foothills these creeks were everywhere. In October, when leaves would fall, the area would come to life, full of color. This image caught my eye because the leaves seem to float above the rocks. A long exposure and small f-stop makes the water like silk.
Toyo 45A   75mm lens.

30 CASCADE ON NORTH CREEK
ZION NATIONAL PARK, UTAH
A hike on North Creek takes you to a place called the Subway. This cascade is about five miles in. I caught the light just before the sun washed out the canyon. A twenty-second exposure and small f-stop gave the water the effect I wanted.
Toyo 45A   135mm lens

31 WILDFLOWERS
TABLE MOUNTAIN, CALIFORNIA
The wildflowers on Table Mountain, in certain years, can be spectacular. Because it is really a mesa and flat on top, it's called Table Mountain. I liked the oak tree because it looked like a bonsai tree. The lupine around it added to the image. As cattle are allowed to graze on the mesa, I was glad that none of them had wandered into my image.
Toyo 45A 90mm lens

33 PARIA CANYON
COYOTE BUTTES, ARIZONA
This place is magical and very popular, but worth the wait for a permit. I was lucky that there had been rains before we arrived; the pool of water makes it happen.
Toyo 45A 75mm lens

34 LIQUID GOLD SUNSET
CENTRAL COAST, CALIFORNIA
Sunsets in Cambria on the Central Coast of California are best in winter. Storms roll through and bring clouds and big surf. At low tide a thin layer of water can reflect the color of the sky, and create a myriad of compositions.
Pentax 6x7 55mm lens

35 WINTER ASPEN
ZION NATIONAL PARK, UTAH
I drove up to the Kalob Reservoir in search of aspen groves. My friends and I found this grove at the top. Light was soft and made exposure easy.
Toyo 45A 360mm lens

36 TOWERS OF SILENCE
DESERT, SOUTHWEST UTAH
Towers of Silence are eroded sandstone; they are very fragile and strange. They are in a remote section of southern Utah and are not easily accessible, but worth it if you can get there. We waited for the light to get to the largest tower, warming it up, but leaving the wall in back in the shade giving it a blue cast.
Toyo 45A 210mm lens

37 WHITNEY PORTAL
HIGH SIERRA, CALIFORNIA
Whitney Portal is the starting point to climb Mt. Whitney. This waterfall is fed by snowmelt; it cascades down maybe three or four stories and can be impressive in the spring. This image is just an intimate part that was still partially frozen. I like the veil effect of the water.
Toyo 45A 360mm lens

38 OCEAN WATERFALL
JULIA PFEIFFER BURNS STATE PARK, CALIFORNIA
Julia Pfeiffer Burns State Park on the Big Sur coast has this spectacular cove with a waterfall that falls into the ocean. The spring flowers, the blue water, and the soft afternoon light make it feel as though you were in the Caribbean.
Toyo 45A 135mm lens

39 ROCKS AND POOLS, LOW TIDE
CENTRAL COAST, CALIFORNIA
This image was made after the sun had gone down. The tide was very low, leaving pools of water around rocks. Every low tide creates different pools and different compositions; they are never the same. My exposure was about three minutes, bringing out the beautiful blue color.
Toyo 45A 90mm lens

40 SUNSET ON THE SOUTH RIM
GRAND CANYON, ARIZONA
I was on the south rim in January, it was snowing and very cold and the Canyon was in and out of view all day. In photography you never know what is going to happen. Just when I thought my sunset image was not going to happen, the clouds broke and the sun peaked though. Ansel Adams said that luck favors the prepared mind; I moved quickly and got my camera set up in time to get this image.
Toyo 45A 210mm lens

42 BURNEY FALLS
NORTHERN CALIFORNIA
Burney Falls in Northern California is fed by a natural spring and is spectacular in the springtime. I only photographed a small section of the waterfall with an old 360mm Tele Zenar. You just can't photograph the whole waterfall, there's just too much of it. I used a slow shutter speed to give the water a gossamer effect.
Toyo 45A 360mm lens

43 WINTER SUNSET
CAMBRIA, CALIFORNIA
Winter sunsets in Cambria can be outrageous. Because the actual sunset was not what I wanted, I didn't expose any film until after the sun had gone down. The color just kept getting better the longer I waited. I finally did some three-minute exposures and was very happy with the results. It really proves that we should wait until the sun is down for sure before packing up our gear. I can't think of all the times I have turned around in my car only to see a blaze of color I missed by leaving too early.
Toyo 45A 90mm lens

44 RETURN CREEK
HIGH SIERRA, CALIFORNIA
This remote section of Yosemite high country is accessible from Virginia Lakes trailhead. Return Creek had lots of flowers and we used it for our first camp on a week-long hike into the area. Mt. Connes looms in the background.
Toyo 45A   90mm lens

45 ASPEN IN SNOW
LAKE TAHOE, CALIFORNIA
I was driving up Hwy 50 near Spooner Lake; it was off and on snow and rain. I saw this grove of aspen out of the corner of my eye. Quickly turning my car around, I raced to set up my camera. I only got a few shots before the snow turned to rain. By the time I returned to my car the rain had washed all the snow off the trees. I have always liked the texture of this image.
Toyo 45A   210mm lens

46 YOUNG SAPLING ON THE MERCED RIVER
YOSEMITE VALLEY, CALIFORNIA
This is another one of my favorite images. This is a spot I go to whenever I am in Yosemite. This spring day the young sapling had just leafed out, the dogwood were blooming, and the Merced River was flowing with snowmelt. I got close to the tree with my 90mm lens, tilted the front a little and got my image. I think it was about a four-second exposure making the water silky white.
Toyo 45A   90mm lens

48 COTTONWOOD BASIN
HIGH SIERRA, CALIFORNIA
A backpack trip that I always like is into Cottonwood Basin in the Eastern Sierra. South Fork Lake is at timberline just below Army Pass. Mt. Langley looms in the background. Lots of great sculptured trees and home to the Golden Trout.
Toyo 45A   90mm lens

49 SUNRISE ON FALL TREES
SMOKY MOUNTAINS, TENNESSEE
I was really looking forward to this photo trip. I had never had the chance to photograph in an area with this much fall color. Even though the locals said it was an okay year, I thought it was magnificent. I scouted this spot the afternoon before, and came back in the morning. The light was just as I anticipated.
Toyo 45A   135mm lens

50 FALL IN THE SAN JUAN MOUNTAINS
SAN JUAN MOUNTAINS, COLORADO
This view is from the road that runs from Ouray to Telluride. Mt. Sneffels is the dominant peak, looming over the valley full of changing aspen.
Toyo 45A   135mm lens

51 SUNRISE AT EAGLE FALLS
LAKE TAHOE, CALIFORNIA
This image happened when I was trying to catch sunrise on Emerald Bay. That didn't pan out so I decided to move over to Eagle Falls. The sun peaked over the mountains and the falls lit up; the two-second exposure gave me the silky water I wanted.
Pentax 67   55mm lens

52 ROCK WALL AND SNAG
ZION NATIONAL PARK, UTAH
This area has some great little side canyons and gullies. The red rock wall was glowing from reflected light. The fall colors and the great old tree snag made the image for me.
Toyo 45A   210mm lens

53 SHELL CREEK MEADOW
COASTAL MOUNTAINS, CALIFORNIA
Shell Creek Road had the best flowers this year. This meadow had a nice palette of color. The afternoon light and clouds created the soft feel of a watercolor painting.
Toyo 45A   135mm lens

55 PINE TREE WITH FRESH SNOW
SIERRA FOOTHILLS, CALIFORNIA
This tree was in my yard in Nevada City. When it snowed, most of the time it melted quickly. I always enjoyed the trees when they had a fresh coat of snow on them. I photographed this pine at sunrise. The pines behind it were getting the warm morning light, while this pine was still in the shade. A couple of hours later the snow had melted.
Pentax 6x7   55mm lens

56 PRIMROSE AND VERBENA
ANZA BORREGO STATE PARK, CALIFORNIA
When the desert gets early rains it usually has a great wildflower display in the spring. This was an El Niño year; flowers and images were everywhere.
Toyo 45A   90mm lens

57 NATURE'S GARDEN
YANKEE BOY BASIN, COLORADO
When I first came upon this field of wild flowers I thought someone had planted them. In my gallery when people are viewing this image, they sometimes ask if it's someone's garden.
Toyo 45A   90mm lens

58 SUNRISE
PORTAGE GLACIER, ALASKA
For me, this shows how things can come together for an image, especially when you have never been to a location and have no idea what to expect. My wife and I were on a two-week motor home trip through Alaska. It was dark when we arrived. We spent the night near the glacier, but never saw it. I got up before the sun and drove to the lake at the glacier's edge. I set up my camera and waited for the sunrise. How lucky I was to have the clouds reflecting in the lake and the soft light! I used a split neutral density filter, and was pleased with the results.
Toyo 45A   90mm lens

59 SUNRISE AT RED MOUNTAIN PASS
SAN JUAN MOUNTAINS, COLORADO
I found this small lake when we were driving over Red Mt. Pass in Colorado. It had a great reflection of Red Mountain. I decided it would look good at sunrise, and that I should come back the next morning. When I arrived, there were no clouds and the wind erased any reflection. Even though it looked like it was not going to happen, I still set up my camera. As the sun came up, the wind stopped and clouds drifted in. Another serendipitous event for the persistent photographer.
Toyo 45A   90mm lens

60 CASCADE WATERFALL
YOSEMITE VALLEY, CALIFORNIA
Winter in Yosemite is always fun for me. This waterfall falls into Cascade Creek. The composition of the rocks and trees with the low clouds gives this an oriental feel.
Toyo 45A   210mm lens

61 PINE TREE AND ASPEN IN FALL
McGEE CREEK HIGH SIERRA, CALIFORNIA
Sometimes compositions just pop up in my mind: this time it was an image of a large tree with aspen in fall color behind it. McGee Creek in the fall is always nice. I found this great old tree with aspen behind it. The sky was like a big diffuser and the colors in the trees popped.
Toyo 45A   360mm lens

63 AGAVE PLANT
CENTRAL COAST, CALIFORNIA
I always thought these were cactus, but they're not. We have plenty of these on the Central Coast, which made it easy for me to find just the right one. I pre-visualized this image with morning light behind it. After several mornings of checking it out, I was able to obtain my desired image.
Toyo 45A   360mm lens

65 OLD MAN'S BEARD
SANTA LUCIA MOUNTAINS, CALIFORNIA
There are many trees in the Santa Lucia Mountains with old man's beard on them. This is not a moss, but lichen, and does not kill the trees. This image is one of my favorites among many in the area.
Toyo 45A   360mm lens

66 MORNING LIGHT AT BADWATER
DEATH VALLEY, CALIFORNIA
2005 was a record year for rain in Death Valley. The salt pan usually has little water in it, but this year it created a five-mile-long lake. Telescope Peak in the Panamint Mountains is mirrored in the lake at sunrise.
Toyo 45A   90mm lens

68 WHITE HOUSE
CANYON DE CHELLY, ARIZONA
I think that Canyon De Chelly is one of the most beautiful canyons in the Southwest and maybe one of the least visited. I photographed from this overlook just before a huge thunderstorm; I had the feeling that at any moment I was going to be struck by lightning. I got the image I wanted and quickly folded up my gear and went back to the car. By the time I got there it was raining very hard and lightning was hitting the ground all around the area .
Toyo 45A   90mm lens

69 FLOWERS AND WATERFALL
SAN JUAN MOUNTAINS, COLORADO
Yankee Boy Basin has become very popular for viewing wildflowers, which makes it very hard to get images without people in them. I liked this spot but there were too many people to make a photograph. I got lucky. Every day we would have small thunder storms and everyone would leave. For me it was my chance. I have a set-up with an umbrella on my tripod and I can photograph in the rain. I got my image with everything refreshed by the rain. A little later all the people returned.
Toyo 45A   90mm lens

70 EAGLE FALLS
LAKE TAHOE, CALIFORNIA
Eagle Falls flows into Emerald Bay, Lake Tahoe. It can be photographed from a lot of angles. It looks different depending on the time of year and the amount of water from snow melt.
Toyo 45A   90mm lens

71 EL CAPITAN REFLECTION
YOSEMITE VALLEY, CALIFORNIA
This is one of my early images. I loved going to Yosemite on Thanksgiving and having the valley pretty much to myself (days long gone). The fall leaves and frozen edges of the Merced River framed El Capitan in the morning light. I liked the abstract feel of the image.
Hasselblad 65mm lens

72 ROCK TOWER FAMILY
DESERT, SOUTHWEST, UTAH
These are so very strange and fun to photograph; there are many different angles for compositions. It is hard to get a size perspective on these without a person in the picture, but the Towers are around three to six feet in height.
Toyo 45A 6x12 panoramic back 135mm lens

73 PARIA CANYON
COYOTE BUTTES, UTAH,
It's hard to imagine these are petrified sand dunes that are millions of years old. We had to be very careful when walking in this area, as the dunes are very fragile. A very wide lens gave me the perspective I wanted.
Toyo 45A 75mm lens

74 THE WATCHMEN AT SUNSET
ZION NATIONAL PARK, UTAH
This is another one of the places in the Southwest where at sunset you will be toe to toe with other photographers. A good image here is not as easy to get as you would think. The right combo of clouds, fall color and good warm light on the Watchmen doesn't come together often, especially when you're only there a brief time.
Toyo 45A 135mm lens

76 CARSON PASS
HIGH SIERRA, CALIFORNIA
When I lived near Lake Tahoe, Carson Pass was one of my favorite areas to photograph. It would be summer at the lower elevations, but spring higher up. Carson Pass seemed to always have good wildflowers. Getting down low with a wide angle lens is a perspective that works well for me.
Toyo 45A 90mm lens

77 OAKS AND THUNDER CLOUDS
SANTA LUCIA MOUNTAINS, CALIFORNIA
The coastal mountains get very green when we have had good rainfall. This particular year was wetter than most. I had been waiting for a weather pattern that would produce big thunderclouds and this day was incredible. I found this great spot.; the oaks were in a field of grass just starting to change color. Because the sky was starting to close in I didn't have much time before it was all gray.
Toyo 45A 210mm lens

78 FALL COLOR
VERMONT
I was photographing this group of trees by a little pond near a road in the mountains of Vermont. After I got my image a person stopped by and asked if I saw the moose. I was so inspired by the patterns and colors of the trees that I never saw the moose. So much for the wildlife photographer!
Toyo 45A 360mm lens

79 GRASS VALLEY POPPIES
SIERRA FOOTHILLS, CALIFORNIA
Poppies in the foothills can be spectacular, with some years better than others. However, you can never be sure, so you spend time going back to the same places every year. A friend and I hiked a couple of miles to get to this spot not knowing if we would find flowers. We were pleasantly surprised.
Toyo 45A 90mm lens

81 OAKS IN SNOW STORM
GRASS VALLEY, CALIFORNIA
When it snowed in Grass Valley the trees were always magical; I had my eye on this spot for some time. This particular day the wind was howling and the snow was blowing sideways. I tried to set up my camera but it just was about impossible. I finally decided to set up in my car! I had to roll the window down to take the picture, roll it back up, clean the snow off the camera, and repeat the process. I have never seen the light like this again at this location.
Toyo 45A 210mm lens

82 SILVER CASCADE
NEW HAMPSHIRE
The combination of rock, water, and fall foliage makes a nice image. This waterfall is easy access from the road and a popular spot when leaf-peeping in New Hampshire.
Toyo 45A 210mm lens

83 SHEEP MOUNTAIN AND FIRE WEED
CHUGACH MOUNTAINS, ALASKA

We were on a motor-home trip in Alaska when I spotted the fireweed with Sheep Mountain in the background. I liked the deep blue sky and the added luxury of the clouds.
Toyo 45A   135mm lens

84 FALL COLOR
NEW HAMPSHIRE

I was struck by the color palette of this composition. The gray tree trunks against all the different colors of the leaves gave it depth. A telephoto lens brought everything into the frame.
Toyo 45A   360mm lens

85 COLUMBINE, SAN JUAN MOUNTAINS
YANKEE BOY BASIN, COLORADO

Spring in the San Juan Mountains in Colorado comes at the end of July at this high elevation. The wildflowers are everywhere and occasional rain showers keep everything green and fresh.
Toyo 45A   90mm lens

86 SUNRISE AT EMERALD BAY
LAKE TAHOE, CALIFORNIA

This image took a long time to get. I was living about an hour or so from the Lake, and needed to get up at 4:00 am to be there by sunrise. Most of the time I wouldn't even know if there were going to be any clouds, and lots of times there weren't. However, this time in fifteen-degree weather, I got my image. It only lasted about five minutes just before the sun peaked over the mountains, then it was gone.
Toyo 45A   90mm lens

88 SACRED KIVA
UTAH

Anasazi Indians built this Kiva. There are sites like this throughout the desert Southwest. Some of them are easy to get to, others are more secret. This one is not visited by most, keeping it from being over-loved. It took me and a friend a few days to locate it. A magical place, it still has the spirit of the Anasazi.
Toyo 45A   75mm lens

89 ANTELOPE CANYON
ARIZONA

Upper Antelope Canyon is another amazing place; exposures of up to four minutes are not uncommon at f-45.
Toyo 45A   210mm lens

90 LIME KILN STATE PARK
BIG SUR COAST, CALIFORNIA

A beautiful Redwood grove on the Big Sur coast, Lime Kiln State Park has a lot to offer: a hundred foot waterfall, (you almost think you're in Hawaii), ferns carpeting the ground, and three creeks which have a silky look from lime in the rock. I bring my workshops here and my students always get nice images.
Toyo 45A   90mm lens

91 STORM SURF
CENTRAL COAST, CALIFORNIA

There are days in the winter on the Central Coast when we get giant swells from storms in the Pacific. These images are from different days; off shore winds and twenty foot surf have an incredible power and energy that seems to hypnotize me. I could spend the whole day just watching the waves.
Pentax 6x7   300mm lens

92 SMUGGLERS' COVE
CENTRAL COAST, CALIFORNIA

This is a large cove with a lot of big rock towers. I hiked down here looking for an image: one with a big wave crashing against one of the huge rock towers. The twenty foot surf was tremendous. Having something in the image to give it size perspective helps make the image.
Pentax 6x7   200mm lens

93 ICEBERG IN MORNING SUN
INLAND PASSAGE, ALASKA

I photographed this iceberg in a small cove in the Inland Passage just after the sun had come up. It looked like a Phoenix glistening in the morning light. I used the small Zodiac from my friend's boat to float around the berg and catch it from all sides. I have a number of nice images of this, I like this one best.
Hasselblad   60mm lens

95 SENSUOUS DUNES
DEATH VALLEY, CALIFORNIA

One of my favorite images of the Death Valley sand dunes, this abstract gives the viewer no sense of size. I like the smooth flowing feel and the monochromatic look. I photographed the dunes in soft light at the end of the day.
Hasselblad   60mm lens

96 SAND DUNES AT SUNSET
DEATH VALLEY, CALIFORNIA

The sand dunes at Stove Pipe Wells are ever-changing; which makes every image a different one. I hiked to the top of the largest dune with another photographer and waited for the light. Even though there had been a lot of foot traffic on the dunes this day, this image doesn't show all the footprints. Hiking to the top of one of these large dunes with forty pounds of equipment can be a challenge!
Toyo 45A   135mm lens

97 TIDE POOL
CENTRAL COAST, CALIFORNIA
The number of images you can find at low tide is endless and ever changing. If you go back to the same spot the next day the image will be different. I usually go at the end of the day when the light is soft and colors are warm. I find, for me, that sunsets are better than sunrises.
Toyo 45A   90mm lens

99 TIDE POOL ABSTRACT
POINT LOBOS, CALIFORNIA
Weston Beach at low tide is always busy with photographers. This composition intrigued me since it is only about a four-foot square area. I like the abstract feel of it.
Toyo 45A   210mm lens

100 THREE BROTHERS AT SUNRISE
YOSEMITE, CALIFORNIA
Winter in Yosemite Valley is a favorite of mine, the light is ever-changing and if you're lucky you might be there right after a snow storm. I hiked down to the Merced River looking for reflections and found this nice composition of the Three Brothers. I would have preferred a sky with clouds, but that's the fun part about photography; it keeps you wanting more.
Toyo 45A   135mm lens

101 HALF DOME RISING
YOSEMITE NATIONAL PARK, CALIFORNIA
After spending three days in a tent at Glacier Point in a snow storm, this was the only glimpse of Half Dome I got. Luckily for me my camera was ready because it didn't last long! I normally don't want contrails in my images, but after that many days tent-bound and running out of food it was nice to know that people were still out there.
Hasselblad 60mm lens

103 STORM SURF, MOONSTONE BEACH
CAMBRIA, CALIFORNIA
Winter brings big storm surf to Cambria. This particular day we had twenty-five foot surf and an extremely high tide. The storm the night before was clearing, creating this monochromatic light. I really had not planned to photograph this spot but couldn't resist the magic of it all. I only shot a few frames with my Pentax. I was pleasantly surprised when I saw my film.
Pentax 6x7 200mm lens

104 LUPINE AND POPPIES
GRASS VALLEY, CALIFORNIA
The Yuba River is a very popular river in the Sierra Foothills. In the spring the surrounding areas can have nice wildflowers. I photographed this spot when I first moved there in 1990 and I think that was one of the best years ever for flowers.
Toyo 45A   90mm lens

105 THE DANCE
WASATCH MOUNTAINS, UTAH
Fall in the Wasatch Mountains of Utah can be spectacular. This image was near Sundance and the valley here goes on forever with brilliant color. No wonder the Indians thought it was a spiritual place.
Toyo 45A   210 lens

107 LAST RAYS
SALT FLATS, DEATH VALLEY, CALIFORNIA
The salt flats at Badwater in Death Valley create patterns that look as if they have been drawn by hand. This was the big rain year, 2005, and the wind was blowing about 40 knots. Keeping my camera from being knocked over was a chore!
Toyo 45A   135mm lens

108 TUNNEL VIEW AT SUNSET
YOSEMITE VALLEY, CALIFORNIA
A grand view of Yosemite Valley, this is probably one of the most photographed spots in the world. I have photographed this many times but never have gotten an image I liked. On this particular fall day the sunset was uneventful, but ground fog came in and some clouds started swirling around El Capitan, which made it more interesting. The ground fog and clouds were in constant motion, creating different compositions. I liked the spots of color from the trees in the valley.
Toyo 45A   135mm lens

109 CARPET OF FLOWERS
SHELL CREEK, COASTAL FOOTHILLS, CALIFORNIA
The flowers in 2005 were the best and it was only an hour-and-a-half from home.
Toyo 45A   135mm lens

110 ROCKS AND SURF
GARRAPATA, CALIFORNIA
This spot's great juxtaposition of rocks makes for nice images from long exposures.
Toyo 45A   360mm lens

120 CRACKED MUD
MOJAVE DESERT, CALIFORNIA
A brave little plant growing in what looks like the driest place in the world. I have always loved cracked mud and thought this little plant said a lot.
Toyo 45A   210mm lens

BC NIPOMO SAND DUNES (BACK COVER)
NIPOMO, CALIFORNIA
I was very lucky this day. The wind was blowing very strong when I first got to the dunes, which made it impossible to take my camera out. However, when I returned in the afternoon the wind had stopped, leaving great patterns in the sand with no footprints.
Pentax 6x7 55mm lens

CRACKED MUD
Mojave Desert, California

Images in the book are available
as Limited Edition prints.
Contact Bill La Brie at his gallery
in Cambria, California:

Visions of Nature Gallery
784 D Main Street,
Cambria, California, 93428
(805) 927-0740
Toll Free: (888) 201-7555
www.visionsofnaturegallery.com